Half-Life

A play

Katy Darby

Samuel French—London
New York-Toronto-Hollywood

Please see page iv for further copyright information

HALF-LIFE

First produced at the Cockpit Theatre, London, in November 2001, with the following cast of characters:

Jay Spencer   Katy Darby
Dirk Shulman   Henry Douthwaite

Directed by Toby Smith

COPYRIGHT INFORMATION
(See also page ii)

CHARACTERS

Jay Spencer, 35, English, female, attractive enough to interest Shulman sexually. A journalist by trade, she is dressed in combat or quasi-military gear. A fast talker and an enquiring intellect: keen and lucid.

Dirk Shulman, 50s, American, male, a former film star turned politician. He wears a well-cut grey suit and quiet tie. He should have the elegant, discreetly preserved elder-statesman good looks of a Paul Newman. Failing that, he must be believable as a one-time silver screen sex symbol.

The action takes place in a cheap, generic hotel room

Time—the present

Also by Katy Darby, published by Samuel French

Open Secrets

HALF-LIFE

A hotel bedroom

A cheap, generic Holiday-Inn-style hotel room, which Jay has hired for the night. There is a single bed with a chintzy bedcover, a wastebasket next to it and a desk and chair. On the desk there are a lamp, ashtray, hotel stationery, mini-kettle, etc. Next to the desk there is a mini-bar fridge stocked with miniatures and water

The Lights come up on Jay sitting at the desk, sideways on to the audience, facing Dirk who is sitting on the bed. Dirk is peeling off a fake beard and moustache. He is awkward, apprehensive and extremely uncomfortable. Jay is relaxed and in control – we'll see why in a minute

Jay Sorry about that. The fake moustache thing, I mean. They would have recognized you otherwise.

Dirk That's, uh, OK. (*He drops the hairpieces in the bin*)

Jay Still, I suppose you've worn quite a few of those in your time.

Dirk Excuse me? Oh, you mean back when I was acting. Yeah, a few. I usually grew my own, though.

Jay Accommodating of you. (*Pause*) I'm not sure why I bothered, really. I don't think the desk clerk looked at us once. And after I'd gone to all this trouble to be inconspicuous.

Dirk I guess he must see hundreds of people in a day.

Jay (*laughing*) In this dump? I sincerely doubt it.

Dirk Then why did we come here?

Jay Couldn't afford anything else. And it's obscure, small; the staff are jobsworths. Nobody cares what you do here as long as you're out by ten.

Dirk Good thing for you, I guess.

Jay Well, yes. (*Pause*) I'm Jay, by the way.

Dirk I'm — well, obviously you know. You can, uh, call me Dirk if you want.

Jay (*indicating the mini-kettle*) Do you want a cup of coffee or tea or something?

Dirk I don't go much on caffeine.

Jay Really? Most people go for hours on caffeine. That's what it's for.

Dirk What? Oh, right. A joke.

Jay Well, it had ambitions to be a joke. (*Pause*) So you don't want anything then?

Dirk Maybe some water.

He moves to get up from the bed and cross to the mini-bar. Jay immediately brings the gun up from the side of the chair — this is the first time the audience has been able to see it — and waves Dirk into a sitting position with it

Jay I'll get it. (*She crosses to the fridge and opens it up, looks inside*) Sparkling or still?

Dirk Sparkling, thanks.

Jay opens the bottle and pours it into a glass, handing it to him, the gun still in her hand

Jay No lemon, I'm afraid. Bloody motels.

Dirk looks at her for a moment, trying to decide if she's taking the piss or serious

Dirk It's really not a problem.

Jay Yeah, I suppose it's the least of your worries at the moment. (*She flips the kettle on and begins unpacking the crockery and equipment for making a cup of tea*) I used to be a waitress, you know.

Dirk Me too.

Jay A waitress?

Dirk Waiter. When I was just starting out. Everybody is, in LA. I was twenty years old, waiting tables at Spago's, waiting to get spotted.

Jay And then you did.

Dirk No, then I got fired for flirting with Elizabeth Taylor. Took me another five years to get my big break.

Jay Better late than never. (*Pause*) I appreciate the fact that you're trying to make conversation with me. It must be quite a change for you.

Dirk How do you mean?

Jay Having to say the right things to somebody else, rather than the other way around.

Dirk Believe me, politics is all about saying the right things.

The kettle boils and Jay begins to make herself a cup of tea

Jay But you know what I mean. Obviously everybody has to kiss arse to the president, but ordinary people — your constituents, your fans – if I were famous I'd never talk to anyone. I'd be worried that they wanted something from me.

Dirk Everybody's got an agenda.

Jay But more so when you're famous. Much more. And the kind of things they want are much smaller — a look, an autograph, a photo — but there are so many of them wanting it the pressure must be huge. (*Pause*) Isn't it?

Dirk shrugs unhappily. Jay's face darkens and she twitches the gun in Dirk's direction

Indulge me by answering. I find this topic fascinating.

Dirk Fame?

Jay That's the one.

Dirk Well then — yeah, it gets kind of wearing. I get sick of being recognized. I get sick of people, some days, but I understand that those people are the same ones who got me where I am, and so I don't bite the hand that feeds me.

Jay That's very — practical of you.
Dirk It's a practical profession.
Jay Which one, acting or politics?
Dirk Oh, both.
Jay Hmm.

Pause. She gets her cup of tea and sits down in her former position, watching Dirk in silence with the gun trained on him as before

Dirk So what is this all about?
Jay Ah, the forty-five thousand pound question.
Dirk Excuse me?
Jay Sixty-four thousand dollars at the current exchange rate.
Dirk Oh. Right.
Jay Silly, I know. It's my way of symbolically reclaiming certain things from under the shadow of America's economic and cultural dominance.
Dirk Like dollars?
Jay Like language.

Dirk looks like he's been told he's about to have his genitals electrocuted. Jay bursts out laughing

My God, you should see your face! I'm sorry; I didn't mean to freak you out completely. I'm not going to put you and your nation on trial for crimes against the English language, tempting though it is. It's just something I do. A stupid idiosyncrasy. That's really not what I'm interested in here.

Dirk So what are you interested in? What's your thing?
Jay What's my *thing*? Why do you assume I have one?
Dirk Because you have a gun trained on me and I don't think you're waiting for an autograph.
Jay Well observed. (*Pause*) Why don't you tell me why you started acting?

Dirk smiles and looks down at the floor, slightly sheepishly. It is a look he has practised both as an actor and a politician, which he

*uses when he is about to admit something personal and perhaps
unwise but ultimately endearing*

Dirk I wanted to meet women.

Jay Go on.

Dirk That was pretty much it, honestly. I wanted to meet and screw
beautiful, glamorous women. And the most beautiful glamorous
women were in LA and on screen so I decided to try and get up
there myself.

Jay Profound.

Dirk No, don't get me wrong. I loved acting. I loved entertaining
people. And when I saw the kind of non-talent that managed to
succeed in Hollywood I thought hell, I can do that.

Jay So you did.

Dirk Right.

Jay And you met a lot of pretty women on the way.

Dirk A lot. Funny thing was, the most beautiful ones were always
waitresses.

Jay Waiting for their big break.

Dirk Uh-huh. (*Pause*)

Jay And why did you give it up?

Dirk You don't know this?

Jay I want to hear it from you.

Dirk What, the set-speech?

Jay If you like. I can't make you say anything you don't want to.

Dirk Of course you can. You've got a gun. You could make me bark
like a dog if you wanted to. I'm surprised you haven't already.

Jay People ask you to do that a lot, do they?

Dirk Only metaphorically.

Jay Oh. Read from the cue cards. Smile at the camera. Toe the party
line. Is that what you mean?

Dirk Politics ain't much different from acting after all.

Jay Except that actors sometimes tell the truth.

Dirk Fair point.

Jay And nobody wants to sleep with politicians.

Dirk You should see some of the letters I get.

Jay But that's different. You've crossed over. They're not aching
to get into your pants because of your farsighted fiscal policy.

Dirk Listen, you're obviously an intelligent woman. You don't
seem crazy or obsessed or dumb. So what do you — I mean, why
are you doing this? What do you want from me?

Jay Tell me why you became a senator and I'll tell you why I've
got you here.

Dirk Back to that, huh?

Jay Till I get an answer, yes.

Dirk OK. I wanted to give up acting because I had been successful
in that field, but I felt I wanted to give something back to the
community. I took up politics because I wanted to make a
difference to people's lives ——

Jay Cut!

Dirk I didn't think you'd like it.

Jay Once more with feeling.

Dirk shrugs

Dirk It's the truth.

Jay You wanted to make a difference and give something back?
What did you take from them that you had to give back?

Dirk I don't know — money, time, caring. When you're a star
people invest a lot in you, emotionally. They want to know about
you. They send you birthday cards, they cry when you get
married ——

Jay They wait outside your house in the dark to watch you undress,
they send death threats to your girlfriends, they write you porno-
graphic fan mail …

Dirk That too. But they only do it because they care.

Jay How endearing.

Dirk The majority makes up for the crazy ones.

Jay smiles and waggles her gun

Jay So far.

Pause

Dirk You're not crazy.
Jay Can I quote you on that afterwards?
Dirk After what?

Pause

Jay Do you smoke?
Dirk I gave up twelve years ago.
Jay That's a shame. You did it so well.
Dirk I had a smoking coach at the studio.
Jay You're joking.
Dirk Nope. He taught me all I know. If you're gonna smoke on
    screen, do it right.
Jay I thought LA was a cigarette-free zone. I thought you got
    arrested for lighting up in the street.
Dirk It wasn't so much back then.

*Jay digs in one of her trouser pockets and comes out with a crumpled
pack of cigarettes. The lighter is in the packet. She offers it to Dirk*

Jay So do you want one?

*He hesitates, eyes on her, trying to guess what would be the best
thing to do*

Dirk Would now be a good time to start again?
Jay Up to you.

*Dirk takes one slowly, puts it in his mouth, takes the lighter from the
packet, lights it and gives the lighter back. He exhales. He looks
good with the cigarette in his mouth — it is movie-sexy smoking,
strictly for the initiated*

Jay You *were* taught well. (*She lights her own cigarette, less
    elegantly*)
Dirk Cancer sticks.
Jay The tobacco farmers in your constituency wouldn't like to hear
    you say that.

Dirk I won't tell them if you don't. (*Pause*) Listen, if you want a
better reason for my going into politics ——
Jay Yes please.
Dirk All right then. Here's an exclusive. I was thinking about my
tombstone.
Jay Why?
Dirk It was a mid-life crisis, a "What am I doing here?" moment.
Jay Ah, one of those.
Dirk You'll find out.
Jay I don't think so.
Dirk You want to hear this or not?
Jay Please.
Dirk I just got to thinking about what my tombstone would say on
it when I died. You know, you see these grave markers with
"Loving Father", "Sorely Missed", "Keen Gardener" and all that
stuff on it. And you have a sense of who they were, what they did,
and you know people will be crying for 'em for a month, a year,
maybe two, and then — nothing.
Jay Nothing?
Dirk Grass grows over the grave, the relatives stop coming, the wife
gets remarried, everybody who remembers them dies. And it only
takes a generation for everything they ever were to fall away. The
only thing left to mark their existence is that damn gravestone.
Jay And what did you want yours to say?
Dirk Not "actor", that's for sure.
Jay Aha.
Dirk There's nothing wrong with that. I loved doing it and I think
I was good at it. But it's meaningless, it's not — in the grand
scheme of things, you are more use to the world as a doctor or even
a garbage collector.
Jay I wanted to be a doctor.
Dirk No kidding?
Jay No. Took the A-levels, Chemistry and Biology.
Dirk What happened?
Jay I failed Chemistry. I aced Biology, which is what you'd think
would matter, but no medical school would take me.
Dirk Couldn't you have been a nurse?

Jay Yes, if I'd wanted to be overworked and underpaid to clean up people's shit for thirty years. If I sound bitter it's because my mother was a nurse and I saw her get screwed every day of her working life. And what's even more interesting is that she died while she was on the waiting list for an operation at her own hospital.

Dirk I'm sorry.

Jay Not your fault. But you can see why I didn't want to be a nurse.

Dirk It's a shame you couldn't be a doctor though.

Jay Not for the great unwell. They were lucky to escape. I would have been a terrible doctor.

Dirk How come?

Jay I don't care about people.

Dirk You cared about your mom.

Jay Different. Other people, ones I don't know, ones I've never met, I couldn't care less about them. I don't have a limitless love of and tolerance for the human race. The vast majority of it just doesn't matter to me.

Dirk is not sure where this is leading

Dirk Oh. Right. So why did you ever want to do it?

Jay Same thing as you. I wanted to do good. I wanted my life to be worthwhile. I wanted to have made a difference, be remembered. And I knew that there are three people nobody ever forgets. The one who raises you, the one who breaks your heart and the one who saves your life.

Dirk What do you do now, if you don't mind me asking?

Jay I'm a journalist.

Dirk I see your problem.

Jay The chip-wrapper conundrum.

Dirk Excuse me?

Jay It's an old journalist's adage: today's news is tomorrow's wrapping for fish and chips. They used to wrap chips in newspaper over here.

Dirk So now I'm hoping this is all for a story you're doing, a kind of "I kidnapped Dirk Shulman" exclusive.

Jay If I didn't write for a pharmaceutical journal you might be right.

Dirk So the photographer isn't in the closet?
Jay No.

Pause

Dirk Aren't you a little young to be having a tombstone moment?
Jay You're never too young to die, are you? The next bus could be the end of the line. Every moment should be a tombstone moment.
Dirk You should be a speechwriter.
Jay And have that written on my grave? I don't think so. And I'm not so young, although thank you for thinking I am. I'm thirty-five. I'm at the midpoint, the fulcrum, halfway through my life. That's if we take the natural span to be the biblical three score years and ten.
Dirk I'm holding out for at least a hundred.
Jay In which case we're both at the halfway mark, aren't we?
Dirk I guess so.
Jay And what do we have to show for it? You have your films, TV, millions of fans around the world, all that kind of meaningless, superficial crap, oh, and a seat in the US Senate. And I have …
Dirk Do I have to guess?
Jay Why not?
Dirk A loving family?

Jay shakes her head, no

A profound faith in God?

Jay smirks and shakes her head

Your health?
Jay We'll come back to that one.
Dirk I give up.
Jay Think how I feel. (*Pause*) I've got nothing very much. I've done nothing very much. Both my parents are dead and I've got no children and currently, no boyfriend. A few friends, a mortgage.

This is my legacy. And it's not enough. I'm like you. I want to be remembered. I don't want my grave to get grown over. I want fresh flowers till the end of time. I mean, ideally I'd like to be immortal, but I'll settle for living on in memory and history.

Dirk So what happened to wanting to do good?

Jay I grew out of it, same as you.

Dirk Who says I grew out of it?

Jay I don't think you ever grew into it, to be honest. I think you wanted to be seen to do good rather than go through the tedious business of actually having to improve anything.

Dirk Oh, if this is about the goddamn environment bill ——

Jay It's not. How dull would it be to kidnap you just to lecture you on ecology? Please. Do you see any tie-dye?

Dirk (*losing patience*) Then what is this *for*, if you don't mind me asking? Why the hell have you got a gun on me in some crappy motel in the middle of Dullsville, England?

Jay Dullsford or Dullchester would be more typically English, but I take your point. Now don't lose your temper, or I might shoot you. I'd rather not have to use this gun but I don't know if you realize how difficult it is to get one in England. It's like trying to buy alcohol in the States if you're under twenty-one, but more so. So you see, it would be almost a waste not to use it now I have it. I had to fill in forms and everything.

Dirk They'll catch you.

Jay That is rather the idea.

Dirk You want to be caught?

Jay No point doing it otherwise.

Dirk Christ, doing what?

Jay Do you want a drink?

Dirk Am I gonna need one? (*Beat*) Yeah, OK, a Scotch would be good.

Jay goes to the fridge and gets a couple of little Scotch bottles out, pouring one each into two plastic glasses. She gives one glass to Dirk at arm's length and they clink

Jay I wish they didn't chill the stuff.

Dirk I guess there's no ice?

Jay looks at him in a don't-push-your-luck manner

Jay As an actor people believed in you, looked up to you, loved you. They trusted you and they wanted you to do well. For the average politician, none of the above applies.

Dirk This is meant to be news to me?

Jay No, of course not, I'm just telling you how I see it. But you used your popularity — their love — to win votes and get into Congress.

Dirk And represent the interests of my supporters, yes.

Jay That's not why they voted you in, and you know it. You're not answerable to them in the same way as other politicians are. They didn't want a voice in the Senate, they wanted a hero. A real American hero to make statues of and name streets after, regardless of what you do or don't do for them.

Pause

Dirk Maybe.

Jay Would you like me to cut to the chase?

Dirk You're the one with the gun. You do what you want.

Jay Where *was* your security, by the way? I couldn't believe you were travelling alone. It's incredible.

Dirk I was meant to be on vacation. I can't relax with a couple of Men in Black shooting at every shadow.

Jay Sorry.

Dirk It's OK. This will teach me to put up and shut up. What do you want, anyway, Jay? Money? A job? Your boyfriend taken off Death Row? Is there some cause or other you're doing this for?

Jay No cause. (*She puts her glass down and begins pacing the room*) Pop quiz!

Dirk What?

Jay It'll explain why I'm doing this, I promise. There are no right or wrong answers; I just want to demonstrate something to you.

Dirk Like I say, you've got the gun.

Jay Exactly. Does the name Adolf Hitler mean anything to you?

Dirk What is this, a joke?

Jay Never heard of him? What do they teach in schools these days?

Dirk No, of course I have. German dictator, nineteen-oh-something to 1945. Little moustache, mistress called Eva, started the Second World War, killed six million Jews.

Jay Very good. Try James Dean.

Dirk (*getting more and more puzzled*) Film star, *Rebel Without a Cause*, died young in a car crash.

Jay Oprah Winfrey?

Dirk Talk show host, actress.

Jay Diana, Princess of Wales.

Dirk Blonde, married Prince Charles, two kids, fashion icon, died in 'ninety-seven.

Jay Very good so far. I'm impressed.

Dirk Thank you.

Jay Edmund Kean.

Dirk Sorry, I don't know. Is he a British politician or something?

Jay No, he was an actor, eighteen hundreds. He was supposed to have been one of the greatest performers who ever lived, but that was before film, so none of his performances survive.

Dirk Oh.

Jay Robert Oppenheimer.

Dirk It's kind of familiar, but … no. Who is he?

Jay Physicist. Father of the atomic bomb. A fellow American. Probably one of the most important men of the twentieth century, certainly in terms of destructive capability. A very interesting guy.

Dirk I'll look him up.

Jay He's dead.

Dirk What's on his tombstone?

Jay I don't know. Maybe something like "You Could Have Fucking Remembered Me"?

Dirk Any more names?

Jay Yes. Lee Harvey Oswald.

Dirk Assassinated Kennedy.

Jay John Wilkes Booth.

Dirk Assassinated Lincoln.

Jay Mark Chapman.

Dirk Shot John Lennon ... Am I sensing a theme here?

Jay I hope so. One more name. Linda Spencer.

Jay Assassinated — somebody? I don't know, sorry.

Jay She was a staff nurse at Addenbrooke's Hospital for thirty-two years. She died last year of operable cancer. My mother. (*Pause*) Do you see the point I'm making?

Dirk I'm not sure.

Jay People you've heard of include film stars, talk show hosts, war criminals, assassins and royalty. People you haven't heard of were some of the most talented or important people of the last century, and I include my mother in that. She was elbow-deep in blood while Diana was modelling diamonds and who did the world mourn for? This is not a vendetta, by the way; I'm just telling you how things are. I think you'll agree that credit is not always given where credit is due.

Dirk I'll go with that.

Jay So where do you think you would be on that list?

Dirk What?

Jay More famous than Oppenheimer? Less famous than James Dean? Take a guess, go on. On my big board of fame, where would you be?

Dirk I guess somewhere between — Lee Harvey Oswald and Oprah Winfrey?

Jay Interesting place to be. And do you think your celebrity is due to the fact that you have done so much good for the people of your native state, or is it just perhaps because you played a lot of cops in a lot of successful films?

Dirk Well, obviously it's a combination of both ——

Jay Don't talk shit. Don't even think about pretending that you're famous because of your arse-covering exercise of a political career. It's because millions of people all over the world have seen you pumping bullets into bad guys. It's because you were sponsored by Pepsi ——

Dirk Coke!

Jay The point is that it's not for any good you have ever done or will do: you could be slicing up babies in your kitchen and you'd still be famous as a good guy. And all credit to you, that's not what you wanted to be remembered for. But I'm afraid that written on your tombstone will be "That Film Star Who Dabbled In Politics". And when the grass grows over it nobody will remember any more.

Dirk (*angrily*) What's your point?

Jay I'm offering you a deal. Like Shakespeare said — who is an exception to my rule of fame, by the way — "The evil that men do lives after them" ...

Jay waits for Dirk to complete the quotation. He stares at her uncomprehendingly

(*Impatiently*) Come on, you should know this! It's the Brando line: "The evil that men do" ...

Dirk "The evil that men do lives after them/the good is oft interred with their bones."

Jay That's right. Listen carefully. I want to live forever. Do you?

Dirk What's the right answer here? I don't know! What gets me out?

Jay Nothing. Dᴐ you want to live forever? Would you like to be more famous than Elvis? Do you want books written about your life, fresh flowers on your grave till the end of time? Do you want your name to mean something a hundred years from now?

Dirk Well, yeah, sure — who wouldn't?

Jay Well, guess what? So do I. But I don't have your advantages, Dirk. I'm not already famous. I don't look good on camera, I didn't marry a prince, I don't host a TV show, I didn't perpetrate the Holocaust. And more to the point, I'm on a clock. I don't have very long. I said I was halfway through my natural span, but I lied because my natural span is going to be a little shorter than most people's, as I discovered a few months ago. So it looks what should be my halfway-point is actually the end of the line. Do you see?

Dirk is visibly shocked. Not only by Jay's revelation that she's terminally ill, but also because of the new context this gives to their encounter and what motive she might have had for kidnapping him. He is getting scared, as well he might

Dirk Oh my good God … I'm sorry … I mean — there's nothing they can do?

Jay They could cut my head off and freeze it, but somehow it doesn't appeal.

Dirk Christ.

Jay There's another meaning to half-life, by the way, which is relevant here. If you've never heard of Oppenheimer I assume you don't know it, so I'll tell you. The half-life of a radioactive substance is the length of time — usually measured in years — that it takes for the radioactivity it emits to drop by half. Are you with me?

Dirk I think so.

Jay So if you walked through Hiroshima the day after they dropped Oppenheimer's baby, you would die of radiation sickness, whereas if you returned fifty years later all you'd get is a higher risk of cancer. Fame has a half-life, like anything else. Other stars shine brighter, and pretty soon nobody can remember who Edmund Kean or Dan Leno or Rosalind Franklin were. The more famous, the longer the half-life. Like if Shakespeare were a radioactive isotope, he'd probably be strontium-90, which has a half-life of several hundred years. Bear with me.

Dirk Sure.

Jay I don't want to die but I haven't got a choice. Everybody dies, some sooner than others. Tough shit. But I want people to remember my name. I want fresh flowers on that grave, or graffiti, barbed wire, poison ivy, I don't care. Because being good doesn't get you remembered. It might get you to heaven if you can be bothered to believe in it but it doesn't get you in the history books. Most people sublimate their desire to live forever by having children. They pass on their genes and their work here is done. I'm told it makes you less selfish. Got any kids?

Dirk No.

Jay Maybe it's true, then. I don't either, as you have probably guessed, so no immortal DNA for me. But I want my fifteen minutes and more, and I'm running out of road. Any guesses at what I'm going to do?

She brings the gun up slowly to point at his head

Dirk Oh fuck, no.

Jay Thought you wanted to live forever, Dirk? Well, here's how.

Dirk What do you want — some kind of suicide pact?

Jay Don't be naïve, I'm not going to kill *myself*. That'll happen soon enough. No. I'm going to ride the wave of my notoriety for the last few months. I'll be up there with all the other celebrity assassins, except special because I'm English and female. Even better, I don't have to feel too bad about it, because I'll know that I have removed from the planet a completely superfluous person who would otherwise have spent his dotage abusing unearned power.

Dirk What's in it for me?

Jay Oh, plenty. You'll get to live fast, die comparatively young and leave a pretty corpse. I mean, there's only so many facelifts a man can have before he has to start shaving behind his ears, am I right?

Pause

Thought so. You haven't got long, Dirk, before you're a joke. You'll never be a grand old man of the screen or the Senate — you haven't got the talent, and you're losing the looks. You left acting at the top of your career — that was wise, but it's all downhill from here. The rest of your life will be lived out in public and the world will watch you shrink and fade. They'll watch you sag and wrinkle; they'll see your eyes glaze over and your hands tremble and little by little the image of you when you were young will fade away. You'll kill your own legend by living too long. Think Marilyn, Elvis, Bogart: dying young is the thing! You're almost out of the zone. I can promise you, after this you'll have untouchable cultural icon status — maybe not along the lines of Diana, but you never actually tortured puppies so I'm guessing canonization *à la* John Lennon or James Dean. It's pretty much win-win, really.

Dirk You think?

Jay What have I got to lose?

Dirk I apologize for saying you weren't crazy. Can I ask you a question?

Jay Yes.

Dirk Why me?

Jay Somebody else would have done it sooner or later. You're such a ripe target. I'm just lucky I got to you first.

Dirk So what, are you going to shoot me now?

Jay Got anything better for me to do?

Dirk laughs, lost for words. It sounds like sobbing

Any last requests?

Dirk Well, seeing as the health risk isn't much of an issue any more, how about a cigarette?

Jay A man after my own heart.

She takes out the packet and holds it towards him gingerly, the gun still on him. Dirk reaches out slowly to take it and suddenly slaps the gun out of her hand and wrestles her violently to the floor, pinning her down while he grabs the gun. He points it at her, still kneeling on her chest or back, panting

Dirk Now don't move a fucking muscle. I'm going to get off you now and I'm going to call the police in a minute or two to come and pick you up.

Jay To take me down to the station?

Dirk No, bitch, to take you down to the morgue.

Jay is genuinely shocked. She had thought he'd turn her over, not murder her. She is white and panicking, out of control for the first time

Jay Christ Almighty, you're not going to kill me, are you?

Dirk Only in self-defence. Get up. On your knees in front of the bed.

Jay gets up and crawls over to the bed, kneeling up in front of it, facing directly out to the audience

Say your prayers.

Jay Say my prayers? What the fuck have I got to pray for?

Dirk I'm giving you a chance to ask for forgiveness. Take it or don't.

Jay Why don't you just let me go? I'm going to die in a few months anyway.

Dirk Exactly. My conscience will be clear. This is revenge, that's all, and because you're crazy and the world is better off without you.

Jay And because you can get away with it.

Dirk That's also a consideration.

Jay begins to cry silently. We can see her shoulders shaking

Jay I'm sorry.

Dirk Pray if you're praying.

Jay Please. I know it's only a few months. But please.

Dirk You tried to kill me.

Jay No I didn't. You didn't give me a chance. Maybe I wouldn't have, you don't know! This is murder!

Dirk No, this is capital punishment.

He pulls the trigger. There is a bang and a smile spreads over Jay's face while Dirk looks at the weapon in horror. She pulls a much smaller pistol from her belly or armpit, where it has been hiding throughout, and points it directly upwards under Dirk's chin. They stay frozen like this throughout the following dialogue

You remember I told you how hard it was to get a gun in England? That one's a replica. It only shoots blanks. Just in case you had your own gun and took mine off me. This one's the real thing. Smuggled over in little bits from my last trip abroad. A Saturday Night Special, I think it's called. Not very hardy, but it does the job. All hail the disposable firearm! What a wonderful invention. I'm glad you're not a nice man, Dirk. I was having a few qualms back there. You seemed so ordinary, just a decent guy. I might even have let you off for good behaviour. Now close your eyes. I'm going to make us famous.

The two of them are frozen in position

BLACK-OUT

FURNITURE AND PROPERTY LIST

On stage: Single bed. *On it*: chintzy bedcover
Mini-bar fridge. *In it*: 2 miniature bottles of Scotch, 1 bottle
    sparkling mineral water
Bin
Desk. *On it*: desk lamp, ashtray, stationery
Chair
Small table. *On it*: teacup, spoon, teabag, milk carton, mini-
    kettle, 3 glasses or plastic glasses
Gun for **Jay**

Personal: **Jay**: cigarettes and lighter, small gun
Dirk: fake beard and moustache

MANAGEMENT OF FIREARMS
AND OTHER WEAPONS IN PRODUCTIONS

Recommended reading:

Entertainment Information Sheet No. 20 (Health and Safety Executive)
This information sheet is one of a series produced in consultation with the
Joint Advisory Committee for Broadcasting and the Performing Arts. It
gives guidance on the management of weapons that are part of a production, including firearms, replicas and deactivated weapons. It is obtainable
from: HSE Books, PO Box 1999, Sudbury, Suffolk, CO10 2WA. Tel:
01787 881165, Fax: 01787 313995. Or it may be downloaded from
www.hse.gov.uk

Home Office Firearms Law: Guidance to the Police
The Stationery Office 2002. ISBN 0 11 341273 8. Also available from:
www.homeoffice.gov.uk

Health and Safety in Audio-visual Production: Your Legal Duties
Leaflet INDG360. HSE Books 2002.

LIGHTING PLOT

Property fittings required: nil
Interior. The same scene throughout

To open: Full general lighting

Cue 1   The two of them are frozen in position   (Page 19)
            Black-out

EFFECTS PLOT

No cues